Praise for *Crash*

"A unique series for childre
-*Booklist*

"Offering kid-authored stories on tough topics like divorce, fear, bullying, and peer pressure, Reflections Publishing opens communication to assist families emotionally, socially, and spiritually. These books are not only fun to read, they're also filled with expert advice, tips, and tools on how to navigate life's most difficult challenges. Must-haves for every family's library, these books are treasures that children and parents can refer to again and again."
-Ken Blanchard, coauthor of *The One Minute Manager* ® and *Whale Done Parenting*

"*Crash!* is an invaluable tool for children, adults, and health care professionals dealing with trauma. With compassionate descriptions of shocking experiences, the book will encourage honest dialogue and offer ideas for anyone helping a child through a traumatic event. The scope of Max's story includes important, often overlooked, aspects of how a traumatic event can affect so many areas and people in one's life. *Crash!* accurately validates that a traumatic event does not end when you are home from the hospital. Any child who is faced with a trauma event would be fortunate to have a resource like this to help them understand that they are not alone, that their feelings are not unusual, and that they can find help and comfort through these most trying times. Bravo, Max!"
- Suzanne Yoder, M.D., Pediatric Surgeon

"*Crash!* is a must-read book for parents, educators, and mental health professionals who are looking for an easy-to-read, user-friendly book about how to explain unpredictable traumatic events in children's lives. Through gentle storytelling, the author encourages relationship-based healing by sharing feelings, creative exercises, and positive thinking to empower children to process the trauma so they are no longer frozen in fear. The 4114U section from multidisciplinary professionals adds a thoughtful, practical game plan. The content of this book supports the notion that it takes a village to heal and grow from traumatic events."
-Mara S. Goverman, LCSW, Parent & Child/Adolesc. Psychotherapist

"Max's story reveals how a pre-teen boy experiences and processes a traumatic event. Through Max's perspective, the reader takes in the crucial dynamics among family, friends, and doctors, that help shape how Alan responds to the crisis. *Crash!* is a must-read for kids and parents who are working through a traumatic event. Teachers, coaches, camp counselors, and anyone who works with kids will benefit from Max's story and the expert advice on recognizing the symptoms of trauma and how to take action."
- Julie Watts, Ph.D., educator, parent, and author

"Good educators, parents, and doctors are always aware of 'teachable moments.' When an event occurs that can have an impact on a child's (or adult's) life, this can be one of those 'moments.' By having a child write his own story and use this as a vehicle to help that child can be extremely beneficial. In addition, by incorporating a guide for parents, teachers, and friends into such books, they will also be an aid to them when dealing with these traumatized children."
- Dr. Richard M. Buchta, pediatrician

"Max Greenhalgh's book, *Crash!*, is a wonderfully written story about a young boy's survival and healing from a very traumatic experience. This book is engaging and encourging. It helps us to understand and gives hope to others who have suffered frightening, potentially life changing events."
- Lewis Ribner, Ph.D., clinical psychologist

"Reading this book really made me stop and think how someone might feel after something traumatic has happened to them. It also illustrates how a person feels on the inside doesn't always match how they look on the outside."
- Aliya Bolt, age 12

"This author does a wonderful job sharing and expressing Alan's feelings. These types of books are so helpful as children experience trauma. We all react differently to traumatic events. *Crash!* is a great resource to have as a starting point for children to work through their personal trauma! Thank you, Max Greenhalgh, for writing about real life."
- Melissa Bolt, MSW

CRASH!

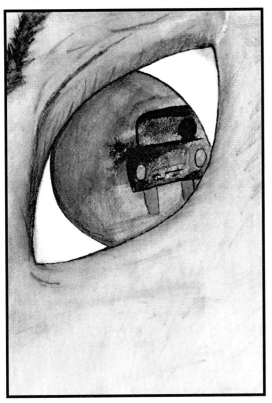

WRITTEN BY
MAX GREENHALGH

ILLUSTRATED BY JESSA WEINER

Dedications:

For everyone that helped me get through my crash:
Mom, Dad, Ally, Scott, Dr. Rubenstein, Mr. Summers,
Ryan, and Andrew. Thanks to all of you.
—Max Greenhalgh

To Max and to all the people who helped him
overcome his fears.
—Jessa Weiner

To Max: It's an honor to have my small part in your
large achievement. What a bright and wonderful
young person you are!
—Scott Weiner, Ph.D., J.D. (AKA 'Dr. Stuart')

To teachers everywhere who meet their children
where they are...every day!
—Laura Stuber

To the One who is more present than we realize.
To my wife, Amy, who is willing to go on an
adventure of a lifetime with me and our three
sons, Brighton, Everett, and Luke. To a life
fully lived with friends, family, and community.
—Josh Kerkhoff

To my loving husband and three beautiful daughters
who support me with my dream to help
children climb over their "rocky mountain"
and discover a rainbow of hope on the other side.
—Colleen C. Ster

Charity:
A portion of sales from this book will be
donated to Challenged Athletes Foundation
www.challengedathletes.org

Sales:
The student author and illustrator of this book
will be distributing a portion of their earnings
into their college savings funds.

REFLECTIONS
PUBLISHING

4114U: How to Read
and Use This Book

Dear Reader,

You may be reading this story for pleasure, or you may have chosen this book because you can relate to its subject matter. Either way, here are some helpful instructions to navigate and guide your way through this book:

1. Read and enjoy the story and notice the vocabulary footnotes; remember the story was written and illustrated by kids just like you. If you have experienced an accident or traumatic event and you are overcoming any fears from this event, then ask yourself if the characters in this story feel the same emotions you have experienced.

2. After you read the story, you will find a section called 4114U. This section has been put together by experts to give you some helpful tips and advice on how to overcome this traumatic event. You will find activities to do by yourself along with some helpful activities to do with a parent or loved one.

Because true healing requires you to focus on your emotional, educational, social, and even spiritual needs, we have divided the 4114U portion of the book into the following three sections:

• Action Steps to Help Families Emotionally
• Action Steps to Help Families Socially
• Action Steps to Help Families Spiritually

One of our goals is for you to feel like this book was written just for you; we want you to see that many other people struggle with life-altering events just like the one you are experiencing. We also want to give you some hope that things will get better, and to empower you (and your parents) by providing the necessary tools needed to deal with overcoming your fears.

While we hope you will find this book helpful, please keep in mind that its content is not intended to be a substitute for any professional medical advice, diagnosis, or treatment. We hope you enjoy this book.

All the best,

Colleen C. Oster

President/Publisher, Reflections Publishing

Acknowledgements:

A wise elementary principal once told me that our job as parents and educators is to teach our children the coping tools they need. By preparing children for difficult experiences like getting bullied or experiencing a traumatic event, then hopefully they will have the tips and tools they need in their back pockets to pull out and utilize when necessary.

This is the mission of Reflections Publishing —to allow children to help their peers through the power of their stories and illustrations, and to allow experts to equip kids with the tools needed to thrive in today's world.

This book would not have been possible without the numerous brainstorming and editing sessions with the following people. I thank you for your many hours of dedication and passion to this mission.

Colleen C. Ster
President/Publisher of Reflections Publishing

Educators: Julia Hinton, Kim Mowry, Erica Rood, and Julie Watts

Business Professionals: Kelley Carlson, Kristina Elliott, MariJo Gleeson, Mica Martin, and Beth Misak

Child Psychologists/Family Therapists: Melissa Bolt, MSW; Lynn Dubenko, Ph.D.; Mara S. Goverman, LCSW; Adria O'Donnell, Psy.D.; Lewis Ribner, Ph.D.; and Linda Sorkin, M.A., LMFT

Student Editorial Team: Aliya Bolt, Caroline Ster, Alexandra Ster, Isabelle Ster, and Ryan Watts

REFLECTIONS
PUBLISHING

Table of Contents

4114U Section

Published by Reflections Publishing
© 2012 Reflections Publishing.

First Edition. Published in the United States of America.

ISBN 978-1-61660-006-8

Visit our website at www.reflectionspublishing.com for more information or inquiries.

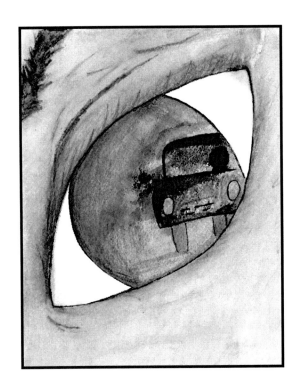

"Courage is resistance to and mastery of fear
—not the absence of fear."
- Mark Twain

Chapter 1:
I NEVER Want to Ride
in a Car AGAIN!

Yesterday's Little League tryouts went well, but it was clear I had outgrown all my gear. My dad and I had just finished shopping at the sporting goods store for baseball gear and were off to Wahoo's Fish Taco, a Mexican restaurant with great fish tacos. A new bat, glove, and batting helmet clunked around in the backseat as my dad made a left turn into a shopping center. I was looking down at my iPod Touch, playing the puzzle video game "Angry Birds," when the car suddenly went over a speed bump. Caught unaware, my last bird flew over a giant green guy and I lost the level. I sighed and tried again.

Once my dad pulled up to the restaurant, it took me a full 30 seconds to realize that we were there. I tucked my iPod into my pocket and jumped out of the car. I caught up to my dad before he went into the restaurant. I don't remember what we talked about—our conversation is just a blur now. That happens before an unexpected event.

When we finished eating, we hustled back to our car, not wanting to miss too much of the action of an NFL game we knew was going on right then. My dad turned on the radio so we could figure out what was happening, and I listened intently. Our car turned onto a wide road that had a spectacular view. On one side of the road, there were houses and businesses. On the other side, there was a fence that if you peered over, you could see down into a gorgeous canyon filled with beautiful flowers and interspersed[1] with tall, sturdy trees. What a beautiful part of San Diego. I had just realized what a perfect day it was—not a cloud in sight, and the temperature was about 70 degrees. As we sped by, I watched the scenery, listening to the football game.

Then it happened.

Suddenly, out of nowhere, a black Ford truck came barreling onto the road. The driver didn't see us at first, as she turned her truck right into our path. Dad honked and swerved left, but the driver thought she could avoid us if she went faster and didn't stop.

[1] interspersed: to scatter among or between other things

The truck hit our car in the middle of the right side. Suddenly, the world was in slow motion. Our car flipped over twice and skidded to the other side of the street, upside down. With tires squealing, metal crunching, glass shattering, and people screaming, I wondered helplessly, as it happened, if it was all a bad dream.

The next 30 seconds felt like 5 minutes to me. I know it isn't possible, but that is the way it felt. Everything happened in amazing detail. I could see the dust flying through the air. I could hear the glass shattering, and saw shards of it fly past me. I could feel the squeeze of my seat belt across my chest. I felt terrified and couldn't breathe. Then everything returned to normal speed, and my dad frantically asked if I was all right.

"Y-yeah, how about y-you?" I replied shakily, suspended upside down. I unbuckled my seat belt and dropped to the ceiling, which was now the floor of the car.

"Oh my gosh," he replied repeatedly from the front seat. He twisted his neck around to try to see me behind him. Bystanders from nearby houses came out when they heard the horrific sound of the crash and were swarming around the doors and windows. A man was rapping on the window, pointing and yelling for me to exit the car on the other side. All that did was baffle me further as to what was going on around me.

Disoriented, I brushed the broken bits of glass from my palms and took a few deep breaths. Finally, I followed his emphatic directions and chose the nearest broken door. I crawled out of the mangled car door. I kept wondering what would have happened if I had been sitting on the other side of the car, where the vehicles collided.

I could feel myself trembling with fear. I NEVER wanted to ride in a car AGAIN!

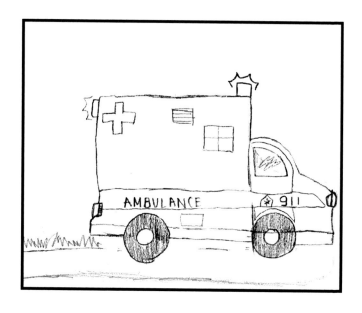

Chapter 2:
The Aftermath

When I got outside the car, reality settled in. I had just been in a car crash! We were very lucky to have so many people nearby who had seen what had happened. I looked back at Dad, who had finally gotten out of the car. People were trying to help him by grasping his arms as he got to his feet, talking to him and reassuring him. He had several cuts on his forehead, a huge gash on his knee, and it looked as if he was having a hard time keeping himself from falling over. Finally, he managed to make his way toward me, though he looked confused and shaken. My new baseball gear littered the street, clearly battered by having been thrown from the car and raked across the asphalt.

A tall, thin man with a serious face walked over to us and took charge.

"I am a Navy nurse and I can help. Someone has already called for an ambulance. It's important to relax and not hurt yourself any further. Lie down on the sidewalk and close your eyes," he directed.

We did what he said, and waited for the ambulance to arrive. As I lowered myself carefully to the sidewalk, I felt a sudden, stinging pain on the palms of my hands. I looked to see what was causing the pain and saw that I had nasty cuts on my hands, three on each one. I didn't know what had caused them at first, but later I learned that broken glass cut my hands. As we laid down on the sidewalk, more people stepped in to help us. One person used her jacket to help block the sun, which was shining in our eyes. Squinting, I also noticed a boy about my age. *This must be disturbing for him*, I thought, and I made a weak smile for his sake.

All around us, I could hear people whispering about the accident.

"Wow, is that car really upside down?"

"The driver of the truck seems okay, but I don't know about these two."

"I was just shopping at the grocery store and I heard the cars collide. It was so loud!"

"Lucky things didn't turn out any worse than they did. Good thing the boy wasn't seated on the other side of the car."

After what seemed like an eternity, the ambulance arrived. To me, it was more scary than it was helpful. The first paramedic who came out checked us for injuries, my first of several exams that day. Somehow, I appeared unscathed except for my hands and a small gash on my elbow. I noticed that my dad kept blinking. I didn't know if he was blinking away tears, disbelief, or if his vision was bothering him.

The paramedics proceeded to load Dad into the ambulance, and I was worried that I wouldn't be able to ride with him. After what had happened, I didn't want to be separated from him. I asked the paramedics if I could come along. They said it was okay, so I climbed in and found a stool that was out of their way. They laid my dad down on an ominous[2]-looking bench with a lot of wires and other medical equipment.

Then I had to endure the long, emotionally painful trip to the nearest hospital. The paramedics told me that they weren't too worried about Dad; they were just being

[2] ominous: something that looks dreary or bad

cautious. I wondered if they were telling me the truth or just trying to keep me calm.

Every time the ambulance took a curve, hit a bump in the road, or accelerated through an intersection, with the alarm blaring, I winced, expecting another bone-shattering collision to follow. It was bad enough to be sitting in an ambulance while Dad was stretched out on the bench, squeezing my hand. His neck was in a brace, so he couldn't even turn to look at me or give me a reassuring glance. For the entire ride to the hospital, the monitors blinked and beeped at us. At one point, I started hyperventilating, and it took a lot of hand squeezing and kind words from my dad and the paramedics to calm me down. I kept thinking about my mom and my little sister, Maxine. I was wondering if they knew where we were, and if they were worried.

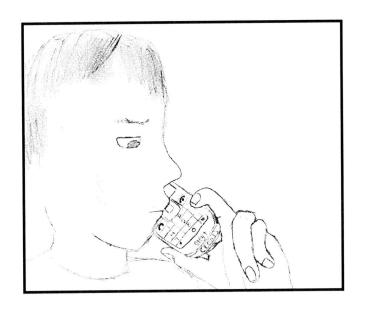

Chapter 3:
The Place of Emotional Horror
(Also Known as the Hospital)

Time really creeps by when you want something to be over. It seemed like hours of silent tears and emotional sickness before we finally made it to the hospital. They rolled Dad into the hospital on a mobile stretcher while I followed, staring in disbelief. I was really scared, but I tried to look brave and in control so my dad wouldn't be worried about me.

They left us in the hallway, which I took as a good sign, because if Dad was hurt badly, they probably would've put us in a real hospital room. It seemed like we sat there for weeks, even though it was about 30 minutes. With nobody to talk to, I became emotional about every 10 seconds. I kept trying to hold back the tears, and keep as quiet as I could. I thought I should be holding it all together for Dad, but he didn't notice because his neck was still in a brace and he was gazing upward. I wondered how it felt to only be able to see the ceiling.

Dad wasn't talking, probably because he knew he couldn't make things better. Now I know what people mean when they say "the silence was deafening." When the doctors finally came to our little stretch of hallway, I was completely miserable. I could only stand back and watch as they questioned Dad, poking and prodding him. Then the doctors gave me a quick look-over. Again fighting back tears, I described what had happened and how I was doing. A nurse cleaned and bandaged the wounds on my hands and made sure all the glass was removed. All the while, I wondered when my mom would get there.

I will never get a job at a hospital. So much panic, desperation, and patients being wheeled around, I thought.

As if on cue, a doctor whispered soothingly to me, "Your dad is going to get a scan now for broken bones and other medical conditions. He wants you to talk to your mom." He handed a phone to me. I guess I had been daydreaming while he had held the phone to Dad's head, and Dad had filled my mom in on the details of where we were and what had just happened to us.

"Alan—are you okay? Is Dad okay? They said you both are fine, but is it true? What hospital are you in?" she asked, not giving me a chance to answer her questions.

I realized that I had no idea where we were and Dad had been wheeled away, so I couldn't ask him. I asked a nearby nurse, and she explained that we were at Memorial Hospital. I relayed that information to Mom, and her reply was, "Oh my gosh, we'll be right there."

The nurse walked me to an emergency room where my dad had been moved. Five minutes later Mom and Maxine arrived. When they entered the room, they rushed over to us crying and hugged us and then did it all again. My mom insisted to a nurse that I be checked for other injuries. Great, I thought, another exam, when all I wanted was to be home. As my mom and I walked to a different area of the emergency room for the exam, I continued to soak in my surroundings. The doctors and nurses all around me seemed to be acting like this was just a routine day at work: pump some air into unconscious people, deal with some heart attacks, and joke with one another in between! I didn't know if that was a good or bad thing, but it was probably good—anything to lighten the mood.

A doctor came over to us, looked at my mom, and immediately asked a question. "Is he the boy who was in the accident with his—" she started to ask.

"Are you talking about me," I interjected, before she could finish her question.

"Oh, so you are him," she said, as she turned toward me.

"Just keep on talking like I'm not even here," I spat.

My mom shot me an agitated glance, but the doctor laughed.

"You're right. Sorry. But anyway," she continued, before I could reply, "on my way to work, I saw the two vehicles on the side of the road or what was left of them, anyway. As soon as I saw it, I felt sorry for everyone involved. I haven't seen one that bad for months. I knew I would be needed soon, so I put a little more pressure on the gas pedal of my car to get over here."

Wow, I thought. I remembered the horrific wreckage we left behind, and the young boy who had watched me lie on the side of the road. I would never look at another accident scene the same again.

The doctor examined me for injuries other than the obvious ones. She didn't find any, but she put fresh bandages on my hands after she was satisfied they were glass-free.

As soon as my exam was finished, I yawned and realized how tired I was. I need to get some rest, I thought, as Mom and I shuffled to the lounge. I lowered myself onto the only couch that was available. I watched the television half-heartedly as my mind drifted back to the car accident again. I began to drift off. *I had gone shopping and I had eaten lunch with my dad. Normal so far. Then I had gotten in a car accident, my dad was injured—wait, what?* I slipped back into the real world when Mom started waving her hand in my face and saying, "Hello, Earth to Alan!"

"Y-yeah," I stuttered, sitting up straight on the couch. "What did I miss?"

"Well, like I said, the nurse just came out with an update. Dad has a concussion." Mom paused. "They want to observe him, to confirm it isn't serious. He is going to need to stay here for another hour at least."

Chapter 4:
My Mind Starts to
Process It All

What? My dad's injury might be serious? I know the car rolled a couple of times, and we came in an ambulance, but...why him? My dad is smart, funny, and passionate for me, Maxine, my mom, and sports. He is one of the best dads on the planet. He takes me camping, encourages me, and supports me when I am having a hard time with things going on in my life. My gut was telling me that the world isn't a theatrical play that always ends with the words "happily ever after," but my heart and mind just refused to accept it.

I managed one word—"Why?" Then, I admit it—I started bawling. All of the day's events had finally caught up with me, I guess. I couldn't hold it in any longer. I sat with Mom and let it all out. Not one of the finest afternoons of my life.

"I'm not finished," my mom whispered, looking around the room to make sure we weren't distracting anyone. "Grandma and Grandpa are coming to pick you up so you don't have to stay here while they finish observing Dad."

I knew what she meant. This place was making my mood go further down on the depression[3] scale. The couch looked worn out from too many tears and sulking bodies. The carpet looked as if a dragon had attacked

[3] depression: a medical condition that makes you very unhappy and anxious and keeps you from enjoying life and things you used to do

it, and the other patients looked gloomy.

My mom squeezed me tight and left me in the crowded waiting room with Maxine. Maxine, only 7 years old and still learning about personal space, squished next to me. But I didn't complain. I was surrounded by people who reminded me of, well, sadness. My grandparents must have raced to the hospital because they got there surprisingly fast. My mom came back to the waiting room, we said goodbye to her, and we headed home.

The long ride seemed to take a day and a half. I rode in the back seat with Maxine, gripping the arm rest. Maxine kept stealing sideways glances, and then turning away to make it seem like she wasn't looking my way. I don't know if anyone spoke in the car—I was lost in my own thoughts.

When I got home, I felt sick. It was Sunday, so I was going to have to endure a week of school, even though I felt traumatized.[4] Football usually cheers me up, but when I turned on the end of an NFL game, I

---

[4] traumatized: to shock someone so much that it takes them awhile to recover.

found it quite dull, considering what I'd been through. We all sat on the living room couches trying to process what had just happened.

It was dark outside when our old garage door emitted a noise like no other on the block, creaking and groaning in protest as it reached the stopping point. I ran out to my mom and dad, happy to see them again. I rushed into my mom's arms, who cried with me. When I saw my dad, I started crying harder. He was still in the neck brace they had put on as a precaution at the accident scene, and his eyes looked weary. I was so glad he was home.

Right before my parents sent me upstairs to bed, I remembered my iPod. I had put it in my pocket, out of instinct, right before the crash. I reached into my pocket; it was still there, almost completely unscathed.[5] However, when I turned it on, it froze on the first screen. I realized that my iPod was a symbol of me—frozen on the outside, but on the inside, things were a lot worse. I had no idea how to fix it.

[5] unscathed: not injured or harmed

Chapter 5:
Back to "Normal" Life

I didn't sleep too well the night of the accident. I kept thinking about what had happened and what could have happened. Even when I did sleep, my dreams frightened me. They were so vivid and horrifying that I often woke up submerged under my blanket, trembling in fear that my latest mental creation of emotional or physical pain was actually real.

The next day, the last thing I wanted to do was to go to school, but my parents were convinced it would be good to stick to my routine and see my friends.

During the drive to school, I realized I was noticing more things happening on the road. I kept pointing things out to Mom: "Watch out for that car over there! Do you see the truck on your right?"

Thoughts began racing through my head. *There was a green light ahead, but it might soon turn red! Why did all of the cars follow so close and seem in such a hurry?* I grimaced when my mom went through a yellow light, jumped at the next intersection when one car honked at another, and clutched my backpack when my mom hit the brakes because of a bad driver in front of her just before we pulled up to my school. I was scared half to death!

When we finally got to school after our

nerve-wracking ride, I slid out of the car and smiled meekly at my mom. Then I trotted up the steps, past the auditorium, before reaching the playground. As usual, Alex, a great friend since kindergarten, was walking toward me when I made it to the place where our 6th grade class lined up each day before school started. I slid off my backpack and strode over to meet him. Alex chattered on about what he did over the weekend, which included watching NFL football games and NHL hockey matches. He mentioned how he thought watching those events were stressful and tiring when the games were exciting and close. The next part of the conversation turned very awkward very fast.

"Guess what I did this weekend?" I asked.

"What?" he responded.

"I was in a bad car accident," I replied. I explained the events to him, which were something I would repeat frequently in the coming days. For a few moments, there was an awkward silence. It was as if Alex didn't know what to say, but it was okay because I didn't want him to say anything about the accident. Alex then started talking as if what I had just said was normal. It must have been pretty crazy for him to hear that from his good friend, but he reacted amazingly fast and well. Next, Alex and I got our normal morning routine started. We talked about school, video games, sports, and crazy things we had heard about; we talked about whatever came to our minds on Monday mornings. I felt much better knowing he knew about the accident, and I realized that being back at school was a good thing.

On most Mondays, our teacher would lead us in stretching and running before class started. When the bell rang, Alex and I jogged over to the basketball courts with the rest of the class where Mr. Winters was waiting. We did our usual stretches, such as touching our toes and standing like flamingos, while I talked to Alex and one of my other friends, Daniel. I told Daniel about what happened, too. Daniel reacted similarly to Alex, and that worked for me. They didn't ask silly questions or say stupid and hurtful things such as, "Cool!" or "Did your car explode?" They thought about my story, and then moved on to a normal subject so I didn't have to keep focusing on the accident. They didn't try to stick their noses into my business. It was only later that I really appreciated the well-judged responses of my friends. I guess I participated in class less than usual, because my mind was distracted at times, but it was a good first day back for a kid who had just been traumatized by a car accident.

There was another problem with Mondays —I had baseball practice. It wasn't that I don't like to play baseball, it was that the field was a 20-minute drive from my house. When I got home, I had a plan.

When it was time to leave, I made sure that my mom could see me, and I made a big show of grimacing when I picked up my bat with my bandaged hands. I felt bad playing up the injury. My hands felt pretty good, and I had even played basketball at lunch recess, but the thought of the car ride there and back made me shiver.

"What's wrong, Alan?" my mom wondered. Then she gasped, "Oh, it must be your hands! If you can't pick up your bat, then you certainly can't go to baseball practice. You're staying home."

I made a big show of complaining about missing one of the first practices of the season, but there was no moving my mom from this decision. As soon as she was out of earshot, I heaved a huge sigh of relief. I was sure glad I didn't have to suffer through the drive after the way the short ride to and from school had gone.

The next morning, I was back in the car again with my baseball cap pulled over my eyes and I squeezed both eyes shut for the ride to school. This was my new way to cope with car rides.

Chapter 6:
I'm the Bad Guy Now

It was Sunday morning, a week after the accident, and I was eating breakfast at the kitchen table. Mom and I had a good conversation about my feelings regarding the accident and the way it was affecting my life. She left for the grocery store as Dad headed to the garage. Apparently, Maxine had overheard my conversation with Mom, because she stomped into the kitchen.

"Why do you get so much attention because of one little accident?" she said.

I shrugged my shoulders and replied, "I don't know."

Maxine sighed. "Why are you so lucky? For the past week, you have had everything that you want. It is like you are king of the family. All of our grandparents are calling you, asking if you are all right—every time I pick up the phone!" She paused. "For dinner, Mom and Dad keep making steak and other foods that you like and I don't, and you have picked all the places we have eaten out. It even happened with dessert. There was one scoop of ice cream left, and Mom and Dad let YOU have it. I am just sick of it!"

"Whoa—Maxine, maybe I have been getting special treatment, but I am hurting more than I have ever hurt before. All the stuff they are doing can't make up for what happened. How would you like it if you were in my position? You haven't seen what I have seen, dreamed what I have dreamed, thought what I have thought, or felt what I have felt. If you can find a way to trade situations with me, be my guest."

Maxine let out a cry of frustration and stormed up the stairs. Just after she slammed the door to her room, tears stung my eyes. We both cried for different reasons that day. Maxine cried because she was jealous and thought her life was miserable and I cried because I felt under attack because of the attention I was receiving.

When Dad came in from the garage, he saw that I was upset. He reassured me and went to talk to Maxine. When he went upstairs to talk to her, I went upstairs, too, and listened from outside her door. It sounded like he understood her feelings, but he also told her how he thought I was feeling and thinking. When I heard his footsteps draw near the door, I darted off to my room and pretended to be engrossed in a book. Next, Dad came into my room and told me that he had now talked to both of us and that he and Mom were available to me and Maxine to support us through this recovery period. He gave me a reassuring hug while saying, "We will get though this as a family. Talk to me anytime."

The next week passed by normally for me, with the exception of being paranoid about other cars on the road, and worrying about car accidents. One afternoon, I knew Mom was supposed to pick me up early, before school normally let out, for a doctor's appointment. She wanted our pediatrician to look me over because I had been having dizzy spells every day.

I thought Mom was supposed to pick me up at 2:00 P.M., but that time had passed and I still sat waiting in class. I started to worry. *Maybe she had been in an accident. Maybe SHE was lying on the sidewalk alone.* Finally, a call from the office came, and I was told to go meet Mom. She had been running late, but was fine. I was so relieved.

Chapter 7:
Doctors, Doctors, Doctors

At the pediatrician's office, I got yet another physical exam and the privilege of describing the "wonderful" event all over again. During the exam, I thought about how much my life had revolved around the accident since it had happened. The kids in my class started talking about it. It came up in conversations with everyone we encountered. My sister heard the story so many times that she wrote a two-page essay recounting the event. Talking about it so much was getting on my nerves, yet not talking about it enough would keep my emotions bottled up. On the outside, I was being cooperative during the exam, but on the inside, my mind was a minefield.

Mom, reading my mind as usual, asked the pediatrician, "Is there anything we can do to help Alan emotionally? He has been acting really bothered since the accident. What might help him to relax more?"

The pediatrician, Dr. Scottsworth, thought for a moment. "You should try taking him to a psychologist to talk about his feelings. I know a good one who I think Alan would like. His name is Dr. Stuart."

"Is something wrong with me?" I asked. "Psychologist? Have I gone crazy? What will they do to me there?"

"Alan," Dr. Scottsworth stated patiently, "a psychologist is someone who helps you with your feelings, and makes you feel more open. Most psychologists are very smart, and I think you will like talking to this one in particular."

"Let's give it a try," Mom prodded. "You can go for as many visits as you want or need, depending on how much you like it."

I shrugged my shoulders and said, "Okay."

A week later, I was on my way to Dr. Stuart's office for the first time. I had gotten over my anxiety about going to see a psychologist, but I still needed to distract myself because being in a car still wasn't my favorite thing. During the ride there, I was searching for a good distraction. My eyes flew to the *Newsweek* magazine on the seat next to me. I picked it up and opened it to a random page. There was a photograph that covered two pages that went with a major story about the tornado that hit a town in Arkansas. The photograph showed a boy who looked about my age holding a younger child while gazing at the wreckage of what I assumed to be his house. If the caption hadn't told me what happened, I never would have guessed that there used to be a house there. It looked like a mess. *What was he thinking? How was he handling it? Was his mom going to take HIM to a psychologist?* I shivered as a more chilling thought entered my mind. *What if he didn't have a mom anymore? Car accidents, tornadoes, hurricanes, earthquakes: so many bad things that can happen to innocent people.*

My thoughts were interrupted as my mom parked our car at an office building not far from my house. We walked silently to the building, both of us collecting our thoughts. Mom and I waited in a quiet lounge for Dr. Stuart to be ready. Soon Dr. Stuart came out to meet us and walked us to his office, which had a desk, a couch, and a comfy chair. I was relieved that there was no medical equipment.

Chapter 8:
Meet Dr. Stuart,
the Psychologist

Dr. Stuart liked to talk, but he also liked to listen too. He was one of the smartest people I had ever met. Our first meeting was not very long. My mom did most of the talking—giving her opinion as to why we were there. It was almost as if I wasn't there. It can be strange to have people talk about you in front of you.

After our first meeting, I met with Dr. Stuart about once a week. Each time, we would talk just a little about the accident, and then we would talk about my life or engage in a debate. Like the tornado survivor I had seen in the magazine, I was looking back over what had happened and trying to make some sense of it, but I was also trying not to dwell on the accident.

Dr. Stuart was one of those people whom you could just hang out with and relax. Soon enough, I was using examples from the car accident in our debates about life, science, or anything else we discussed. Dr. Stuart also had subtle suggestions about getting through something like this. He encouraged me to talk to my parents about how I was feeling, and to go out and have fun with my friends. Who knew that playing video games with the guys would be therapeutic—getting back to the normal things felt great.

Dr. Stuart complimented the way I was handling the accident and the aftermath. This gave me a sense of pride, and I started to see how I gained something from the accident and I was stronger because of it.

Dr. Stuart helped me get used to talking about my feelings regarding the accident. It became part of my life and memory forever, but not my only focus.

Chapter 9:
No Longer Frozen

Over time, I started to feel better. My focus on the accident faded, though I still thought about it sometimes and I started writing about it. I would write in my school journal about all the things that happened on the day of the accident or how I was dealing with my feelings about the accident as I tried to get back to normal life each day. When

Mr. Winters asked our class to write about a personal experience. I wrote about the accident, which I think he liked because so many of the other stories were about the same things, such as trips to Disneyland and learning to ride a bike. I am pretty sure he doesn't get a lot of stories about cars flipping over and the drama of the emergency room. I even wrote a fictionalized story about the accident in my spare time. Writing helped me organize how I felt, and it made my tale much easier to tell.

Riding in a car got better too. For one thing, I stopped closing my eyes while I was riding in the car. I realized that I was missing out on way too much that was going on around me. Before the accident, I was an oblivious passenger—never really paying attention to my surroundings. Now, I like to watch what is going on, and I am not afraid. Believe it or not, I think the accident was a positive experience because I learned how to cope with trauma and I have more awareness on the road. Both of these things will help me when I am older. My iPod is no longer frozen, and neither am I.

4114U
(Information For You!)

Written by:
Scott Weiner, Ph.D., J.D. - Clinical Psychologist
Laura Stuber, NBCT - Sixth-Grade Teacher
Josh Kerkhoff - Religious Scholar

Kids: Our intent is that you will read through this 4114U section with your parent or guardian. Please read and discuss the tips and tools provided as you process this information together. Our goals are for you to create a game plan that will help you navigate through the traumatic event that you experienced.

Parents: A parent's job is to give their children the tools needed to navigate, and to be active participants in solving problems that will invariably come their way in life. Experiencing trauma and fear can be scary and overwhelming for a child, and by reviewing the following pages together, you can develop a game plan of action.

Hopefully, this book will open up a wonderful world of communication where you and your child can safely navigate through this tough situation together as a family.

Action Steps to Help Families Emotionally

Written by:
Scott Weiner, Ph.D., J.D. - Clinical Psychologist

 WHEN LARGE, BAD THINGS HAPPEN

Hello! "Dr. Stuart" here. This is a message for certain YOUNG PEOPLE…this might mean you if you're reading this.

Let's talk first about two kinds of LARGE bad things. All bad things feel large when they happen, so it's hard to tell the really bad ones sometimes. In this story, Alan knew it was bad when he had to pull his hat down over his eyes to ride in the car…in the car, get it?

REPEATING something made it clear to him. It was a problem, and a VERY SMART and caring Mom got Alan to go to a psychologist to talk about his feelings. This was a PUBLIC, LARGE, BAD THING. He got help, and he's now OKAY. Public, Large, Bad Things can be incredibly large sometimes, like natural disasters and so on. It seems that there is never enough help. That's the bad news. But the good news, if we can call it that, is that EVERYBODY KNOWS there's a problem. Help is probably on the way.

Kids: WHEN PRIVATE, LARGE, BAD THINGS HAPPEN

Often worse for young people, and VERY common, are PRIVATE, LARGE, BAD THINGS. Children suffer in silence, sometimes feeling afraid, sometimes embarrassed, sometimes feeling guilty —yes, get that—blaming themselves when it's not their fault!

Doesn't seem fair—because it isn't. But it goes on and on. Or maybe you think it's no big deal... like you're a wimp for complaining...other people have it worse, right? Maybe...but if it's making life feel awful, better to deal with it.

Making your life worse does not help the other guy who has it worse than you. HE should speak up too. And it gets complicated. What if a THING happens to a friend and you've promised not to tell? WHAT SHOULD I DO? I PROMISED!

Kids: WHEN PUBLIC, PRIVATE, BAD THINGS HAPPEN

Next are those strange ones, that are PUBLIC but nobody talks about it. That's like bullying, or when groups of kids gang up and embarrass a particular young person because she or he is different, or vulnerable. It's cruel behavior; we see it everywhere—even in the animal kingdom, for that matter. Well, like many things in the private, bad thing department, the solution is easy to say, but hard to do, because of those FEARFUL, SHAMEFUL, EMBARRASSED feelings. But here's what to do:

TELL SOMEBODY!

Go ahead. Mom, Dad, teacher, doctor, someone. Good grown-ups can be quite useful sometimes. We WANT to help. We'll even help you handle the fact that you told someone when you promised you wouldn't tell a soul.

Now, let's say the grown-up says, in a nice tone, "Oh, that's just an exaggeration," or "He wouldn't do that...why...I've known him for years!" Then try the teacher, nurse, or professional person. OKAY. You get the message. And one more thing:

DON'T WAIT.

I see people in my office who wait 20, 30, or 40 years. Half a lifetime. Please don't wait. Please. Relief is sitting right before you, within reach. You just don't know it yet—like just out of view, just around the corner.

GAME PLAN
FOR THE GROWN-UPS

What should I look for? How do I be sure my young ones are safe? We're so busy. These lives we lead—many are so overworked. Moms and Dads and careers and challenges and long hours. The kids are living in a virtual electronic world. Many (but not all) of you would be astounded to see the texts and pictures sent between young people. We can be so oblivious while so well-intended.

Other than the PUBLIC bad things (see the kids section), your child, my child, all of them are very likely to try to hide traumatic occurrences, out of shame and fear of weakness. Stoicism can seem so virtuous and admirable. However, believe me: Trauma can bring a Titan to his knees, and break his life. And our children? They may actually "out-survive" the traumatized adult, but at huge sacrifice. Trauma is an evolving area of study. In developing brains, the traumatic event can develop its own rhythm, like the formation of a deeply imprinted habit. Give it a year or so to percolate underground, and very intractable thought-feeling-action clusters are formed that can overdetermine a young life's path, leading one to search for relief in equally intractable forms.

PTSD (Post Traumatic Stress Disorder) is so very real, and of such profound impact. Just to illustrate: Suppose we put a person in a condition of extreme emotion in the presence of an intense event that rivets the senses, in a condition in which he/she feels virtually no control? External to this person is all perceived power and authority—in all, these are prime conditions for hypnotic suggestibility. It just may be that trauma is a form of trance whose recurrence is nearly irresistible in the presence of sensory repetition. The author, riding in the car, again, for example.

Gentle, supportive interference with these patterns is the province of the therapist. New therapies are emerging for trauma treatment. Any responsible therapist will give a patient or his/her parents a set of choices and/or referrals if it is outside that therapist's sphere of work.

What, again, do I look for?

Change.

Watch for change, any furtive distancing without explanation, large moves away from former friends, extreme emotion where there was none before in response to a person or event. You may be laughing aloud now—My child is ALWAYS like that! I hear you say. I don't mean the normal adolescent part —remember when we realized our poor parents were hopeless adults, and we'd be caring for them in a few short years? Their scorn is not what I'm referring to.

Rather, there could be a flat cast to the look in his eyes, a retreat from what used to please him or her, a decision not to be with friends or a late-breaking decision to avoid a family gathering that was formerly her great pleasure.

What 2 Watch 4

- Nightmares
- Extreme jitters
- Loss of pleasure in life
- A large turn for the worse
- More fear of the new
- Loss of appetite
- Odd reversions to clinginess
- New health problems that seem to have no basis in history or fact
- Sudden drop in school concentration or focus

When the above items show up, it's time to get help, and as I told the kids:

Don't Wait.

Game Plan: What to Do?

Kids & Parents: **Action Steps for Families**

Regular daily discussions. Don't be put off. Join in the laughter about how very out of it you are. And believe me—YOU ARE. (If I have to be, so do you!) And I guarantee my child could lay it out—up, down, and sideways—how over the hill I am.

Stay close, so close—a few specifics: computers, televisions, iPads, and so on. Also, is there really a need for a television in a bedroom? Really? I can tell you this. I've met a good number of 2300+ SAT kids, and a few 2400's. No television in the room. I guarantee it. Not that that is the gold standard, the be-all and end-all, but it's not so common to turn Harvard down, now is it?

How to Process Trauma/Fear

Experiencing trauma and fear can be very upsetting. Use the space below to write out your fears and discuss with a parent or guardian different ways to overcome your anxiety of the event. If you can come up with creative ways to address these anxious feelings ahead of time, then you will be better prepared when you do have them and have the necessary tips and tools in your back pocket to pull out and utilize. Use the writing and drawing space below to process the event and any images in your mind that are still bothering you.

Action Steps to Help Families Socially

Written by: Laura Stuber, NBCT,
Sixth-Grade Teacher

Children who have experienced a traumatic event may need their parents' and teachers' time, patience, and support as they work through their feelings. As with adults, children will vary in their response to trauma. Some children may exhibit few if any signs of distress; others may show signs and work through the process in a few days or weeks; and still others may show no signs at first, only to have behavior problems pop up weeks or even months later.

If family members or others were involved in the traumatic event, be aware that the child may have concerns about their safety and welfare as well. He/she may also have feelings of guilt, believing that he/she somehow caused the accident or crisis situation. All of these reactions can leave a person feeling emotionally drained and physically exhausted.

Just like you would study for a math test, you need to focus on ways to overcome this traumatic event. Just like math, some steps and concepts are easier than others to master, but before you can fully recover and heal from your emotional injuries, you need to put the time in to get the A+. So let's get you prepared!

Tips for Parents and Teachers

How to Earn the A+
for Awareness of Possible Reactions

For any adults in the child's world, being aware of the possible reactions to a traumatic event is the first step to being supportive. Keep in mind that a child experiencing stress due a traumatic event may:

- re-experience the event through nightmares or flashbacks
- avoid people, places, or activities that trigger memories of the event
- have raw feelings: be fearful, emotional, irritable, jumpy, or on edge

What 2 Watch 4

Some reactions that may signal stress or anxiety in an elementary-aged child are:
- more than usual distractibility
- refusal to comply with normal requests
- changes in activity level (increase or decrease)
- physical aggression toward siblings or peers
- stomachaches
- change in eating habits
- isolation from friends, social situations, the world
- regressive behaviors, i.e. need to have a light left on or door cracked open at bedtime

How to Earn the A+ for Acceptance of Feelings

People feel what they feel—period. Following a traumatic event, people may feel things in certain situations that they didn't feel before. A child's fears may not make sense to you, but they are part of his/her reality. Do not judge or attempt to correct these feelings. If you remember that "feelings" are not "rational," you will be able to respond in a way that may be more helpful to the child.

Before your child returns to school, let his/her teacher know about what happened. A phone call or even just a quick e-mail will give the teacher a heads up.

You will obviously want to make time to talk with your child about his/her feelings during this time. Invite your child out for some one-on-one time for a smoothie or a walk on the beach. Or allow a few extra minutes at bedtime for checking in with your child.

Teachers, if the child wants to talk with you about his/her experience, make some time on the way out to lunch, walking in to school in the morning, or talking for a few minutes together after school. A sympathetic ear will go a long way in supporting the child through this time. Listen to and accept the child's feelings—fears, anxiety, and all.

Teachers:

How to Earn the A+ for an Action Plan at School

Teachers, upon the child's return to school from a traumatic event, discreetly let him/her know that you are aware of his/her recent experience. The child might not be comfortable with his/her peers knowing about it yet—respect these feelings.

#1 Keep lines of communication open with your student's parents. Keep them posted about your observations regarding any changes in the child's behavior. Check in with parents about anything they are hearing at home.

#2 Stick to classroom routines and schedules as much as possible. This will help with the child's sense of security as he/she works through the trauma.

#3 Invite the school psychologist to class. Let him/her know about the child's recent experience ahead of time and see if he/she can facilitate an appropriate lesson or activity. Chances are, other kids have had traumatic experiences that they have dealt with, too, and this could be therapeutic for them as well.

#4 Weave a few read-alouds into your teaching over the next few weeks that have themes of dealing with challenges or overcoming fear; allow time for group discussion afterward. Set a tone of compassion and caring. Don't get "preachy" about how you think such situations "should" be handled.

#5 Depending on your schedule and your daily routine, offer a writing workshop with the students' choice of writing topic as a definite part of your curricular activities for the next few weeks. The child may use that time to write about and process the traumatic event.

#6 Incorporate stress reduction activities into the school day. Try periodic times for stretch breaks or for practicing relaxation techniques. Try doing yoga once or twice a week at P.E. If you don't feel qualified to teach it, maybe you could join with another teacher who can teach it while you help with class management and support.

#7 Be flexible with classroom discipline. While you cannot let rude or aggressive behavior go unaddressed, you may be able to find effective yet gentle ways to deal with outbursts or refusals to comply with classroom expectations.

As a teacher, your awareness, acceptance, and appropriate action will go a long way in supporting the child as he/she works through the stress of a fearful or traumatic event.

Kids:

How to Earn the A+ for Awareness of Possible Reactions

It might be helpful for you to know that a traumatic experience can take a while to work through. You may look and feel fine on the outside, but you may have some healing to do on the inside. You can think of it as a bruise on your emotions. Like a bruise on your body, there is no bleeding or scabbing on the outside, but you are bleeding a little on the inside just under the skin. You can't put Band-Aids® or ice on the outside to heal your bruise. You have to give it time, and your body will heal the bruise from the inside out. The same is true of this trauma bruise. Give it time, and you will heal from the inside out.

It might also be helpful for you to know that you may feel anxious or afraid after a traumatic event. You may be a person who has flashbacks to the event, and you may know exactly what you're worried about. Or you may be a person who doesn't have flashbacks, but you may have a nervous feeling from time to time and not know why. These are different ways of feeling anxious. It can help a bit just to be aware of these feelings of anxiety.

When you are aware of feeling anxious, try closing your eyes for a few seconds and getting in touch with any stress in your body. Are your shoulders tense? Do you have a stomachache? Do you feel like running away? Sometimes just saying, "I'm feeling anxious right now" can help take the edge off those feelings.

Remind yourself that you had a traumatic thing happen to you and that it's normal to feel anxious afterward. Accept your feelings and remind yourself that you will feel better with time. Use the space below to create a game plan.

My Game Plan

REFLECTIONS
PUBLISHING

A+ Report Card
Did You Make the Grade?

Kids:
- ☐ I have open communication with my parents.
- ☐ I have talked to my teacher(s) to make them aware.
- ☐ I am aware of how I am feeling and acknowledge those feelings.
- ☐ I accept my feelings and know things will get better.
- ☐ I am focusing on ways to overcome my fears.

Parents:
- ☐ I have notified the teacher.
- ☐ I have let go of any guilt I am carrying from the accident.
- ☐ I am talking to my child and letting him/her know that I am available to support in any way possible.
- ☐ I am keeping our family in a routine schedule.
- ☐ I will purchase a journal for my child to process his/her thoughts in writing.

Teachers:
- ☐ I am keeping the lines of communication open with parents and child.
- ☐ I am sticking to class schedules and routines.
- ☐ I have notified the school psychologist.
- ☐ I am reading books in class on the topic.
- ☐ I am giving the students time to journal in class.
- ☐ I am being supportive of the student's behavior during this recovery time.

Role-Playing Script for:

Overcoming Fear of a Car Accident

Comic Drawings by: Garrett Richie, age 12

Action Steps to Help Families Spiritually

Written by: Josh Kerkhoff
Solana Beach Presbyterian Church
Next Generation Pastor

When a person goes through a difficult time in life, they may question their belief system and wonder why this bad thing is happening to them. Research from academic and medical journals has shown that when people are faced with life challenges or health problems, it is the individuals who have a strong belief system that have the best overall, positive recovery. When a person believes in something or someone bigger than themselves, then they can heal faster and experience less pain.

Even though the circumstances of your situation may seem overwhelming and you may feel uncertain of God's presence, God is with you. It is good to have friends and family who can be present with you, often without even having to say a word, to remind you of God's presence. Nobody—adult or child—is strong enough to go through life on their own. Having a strong connection with trusted friends and adults and a belief system can help you process and reflect on a difficult experience and continue to heal.

A number of years ago, my wife and I experienced a tragic loss (a "crash" of sorts where no one was at fault). Deep inside, we felt incredible pain and loss. Just moments after discovering the bad news, we were driving away in our car and the only thing we could do was sob and cry, letting emotion out that was buried deep within.

It was not what we expected, it was out of our control, we didn't know who to blame or if there was anyone to blame, but we were experiencing great pain and we didn't know if anyone else could relate.

It took some time for us to know what we were experiencing and how to journey through it. At different places in our lives and in different ways, all human beings experience pain and loss. This is one of the things that unites us as humans, and all of us travel through these experiences in different ways.

In our pain and loss, we were left asking, where is God? Where is God in the midst of this "crash"? Where is God in the midst of this dark journey?

Some people believe that God is distant and more of an object than a subject. Others might say that God is present in all created things. What I have come to know and trust is that God is closer than we all have the ability to see and hear. God is present in the midst of our pain and loss, in the midst of our "crashes" and dark journeys. There are signs of God's presence all around us in people and in creation. Sometimes it is through the pain, the "crashes" of life and dark journeys, when we come to know God.

We have different experiences and stories, yet in and with us, God is present!

If you have experienced a "crash," what does it mean for you that God is present with you and others? When it comes to others who experience their own "crashes" and accidents, what would it mean for you to be present through their experiences? How might you be with them in the midst of their pain? Do you feel like you need to say something? Why do you feel like you need to say something to comfort them?

When you experience "crashes," you may discover the importance of community, and when others experience similar things, you may be able to be their community.

Prayer:
"God, thank you for your presence in and through all of our experiences in life. You are with me in the highs and lows; you are with me when I am celebrating great joys and afraid of what has just happened or what will take place next. I pray for friends and family that will be with me like you are always with me. As I turn to others, may I also be present to others. Amen."

Affirmation Exercise:

Preserve your sense of confidence, worth, and self-esteem by writing a list of positive statements as a reminder that you are not defined by this event. By focusing on your strengths and who you want to become, you will feel the momentum that will push you directly through challenging and stressful life experiences—ultimately helping you heal.

You can hang this list in your locker, post it on your mirror, or write it in your journal.

Daily positive affirmations:

- I am a good student.
- I am a loyal friend.
- I am a creative writer.
- I like myself and who I am becoming.
- I have goals that I want to achieve.
- My dream is to be_____.

GRATEFUL JOURNAL

Journal Ideas:
- Write something you are grateful for or makes you happy every day.
- What are your goals?
- A special trip coming up.
- Plans for the summer.

About Our Experts:

• Josh Kerkhoff
Solana Beach Presbyterian Church
Next Generation Pastor

Since 1999, Josh has worked with students sharing faith through the community of the local church. For the past six years, he has served with SBPC as he encourages, supports, and leads change in their focus with children, students and their families, and young adults. One of his passions is to help people see the interconnected stories and images that are woven through their often segmented lives. Josh has a Master of Divinity degree from Fuller Theological Seminary in Pasadena, CA, and is pursuing his Doctor in Ministry through George Fox University in Newberg, OR. He lives with his wife, Amy, and three boys, Brighton, Everett, and Luke, in Encinitas, CA. To keep up with him, you can follow him on twitter @joshkerkhoff and receive occasional updates at: http://joshkerkhoff.wordpress.com/.

• Laura Stuber, NBCT
Solana Beach School District
Sixth-Grade Teacher

Laura Stuber has been in education for 30 years. She has worked with parents and toddlers, preschoolers, and early elementary -age students and is currently teaching sixth-graders at Solana Pacific Elementary in Solana Beach, CA, and loving it! Laura has a B.A. in Liberal Studies with minors in Child Development and Psychology, and a Multiple Subjects Teaching Credential. She believes that education is a lifelong process and recently achieved National Board Certification in Literacy. Laura lives with her husband in north San Diego County. They have three grown children and a new grandbaby nearby.

· Scott Weiner, Ph.D., J.D.

Clinical psychologist and attorney practicing and residing in San Diego's North County

Dr. Weiner's therapeutic style is highly eclectic. He uses every means he can imagine to understand and reach his patients. He will crawl about with your 4 year-old; exchange stories with an older child; help an adult address and modify a troubling thought-behavior problem; aid an executive to understand and change the culture of the workplace; or explore life, death, and eternity with an elder. Kindness, humor, understanding, and love of living are touchstones in his practice.

First trained in Communications and Group Dynamics at Carleton College and the University of Minnesota, Dr. Weiner was an early instructor in the Minnesota Couples Communications Program. He pursued doctoral study in Clinical Psychology at USIU in San Diego, finishing his Ph.D. in 1984, and was first licensed in 1986. He interned at Alvarado Hospital in San Diego, and has 30 years' experience working with diverse clinical populations. In 1999, Dr. Weiner took sabbatical to attend USC Law School, and joined the California Bar in 2003.

He lives in Del Mar with his wife (and superb therapist), Lorraine; his daughter; and Dog-Without-Peer, Charlie, the golden retriever (a remarkably fine therapist in his own right).

Web Links:

- AskMen - Master Fear
  http://www.askmen.com/money/body_and_mind/
  3_better_living.html

- CTRN: Change That's Right Now
  How to Overcome Accident Fear
  http://www.changethatsrightnow.com/accident-fear/
  how-to-overcome/

- eHow.com - How to Overcome Fear After a Car Accident
  http://www.ehow.com/how_6110612_overcome-fear-after-
  car-accident.html

- FearofStuff.com - Fear Of Driving - Help for Fear Of
  Driving - Phobias
  http://www.fearofstuff.com/travel/fear-of-driving/

- Giftfromwithin.com
  http://www.giftfromwithin.org/pdf/crash.pdf

- Joyce Meyer Ministries - Overcoming Fear
  http://www.joycemeyer.org/articles/ea.aspx?article=
  overcoming_fear

- Psychology Today - Overcoming Fear
  http://www.psychologytoday.com/collections/201106/
  overcoming-fear

- Raminader.com
  Patient Handout for Overcoming Driving Fear and Avoidance
  http://www.raminader.com/ptsd_resources.htm

- Streetdirectory.com
  http://www.streetdirectory.com/travel_guide/58519/
  car_accidents/how_to_prevent_car_accidents.html

- WikiHow - How to Overcome Fear: 12 steps
  http://www.wikihow.com/Overcome-Fear

References for Adults:

- Blanchard, Edward B. , Ph.D., ABPP, and Edward J. Hickling, Psy.D. *After the Crash: Psychological Assessment and Treatment of Survivors of Motor Vehicle Accidents, Second Edition.* Washington, D.C.: American Psychological Association, 2003.

- Bryant, Richard A., Ph.D., and Allison G. Harvey, Ph.D. *Acute Stress Disorder: A Handbook of Theory, Assessment, and Treatment.* Washington, D.C.: American Psychological Association, 2000.

- Farber, Adele and Elaine Mazlish. *How to Talk So Kids Will Listen & Listen So Kids Will Talk.* New York: Harper Collins, 1980.

- Koenig, Harold G., M.D. *The Healing Power of Faith: Science Explores Medicine's Last Great Frontiers.* New York: Simon & Schuster, 1999.

- Roizen, Michael F., M.D., Mehmet C. Oz, M.D., and Ellen Rome, M.D. *You: The Owner's Manual for Teens: Guide to a Healthy Body and Happy Life.* New York: Simon & Schuster, 2011.

References for Kids (Grade Level):

- Andrews, Beth, LCSW. *Why Are You So Scared?: A Child's Book About Parents with PTSD*. Washington, D.C.: Magination Press, 2011. **(PreK-2)**

- Doman, Mary Kate. *Blizzard*. Costa Mesa, CA: Saddleback Educational Pub., 2012. **(K-3)**

- Doman, Mary Kate. *Crash*. Costa Mesa, CA: Saddleback Educational Pub., 2011. **(PreK-2)**

- Holmes, Margaret M. *Terrible Thing Happened: A Story for Children Who Have Witnessed Violence or Trauma*. Washington DC: Magination Press, 2000. **(PreK-2)**

- Kaufman, Gershen, Ph.D., Lev Raphael, Ph.D., and Pamela Espeland. *Stick Up For Yourself*. Minnesota, MN: Free Spirit Publishing, 1999. **(4-5)**

- Meyer, Joyce. *Battlefield of the Mind for Kids*. New York: Faith Words, 2006. **(K-6)**

- Meyer, Joyce. *Battlefield of the Mind for Teens*. New York: Faith Words, 2006. **(7-12)**

- Price, Mathew. *Little Red Car Has an Accident: A Pop Up Book*. Dallas, TX: Mathew Price, Ltd., 2009. **(K-3)**

- Tompkins, Michael A., Ph.D., and Katherine A. Martinez, Psy.D. *Anxious Mind: A Teen's Guide to Managing Anxiety and Panic*. Washington, D.C.: Magination Press, 2009. **(7-12)**

In-Depth 4114U Concepts:

Book Club Discussion Questions:
Written by: Max Greenhalgh

1. Have you ever had a traumatic experience like Alan's? What emotions did you feel right after it happened?

2. Alan's friends didn't ask a lot of questions about the accident. He seemed to be glad about that. Do you think you would want your friends to keep talking about something that happened to you? What would you say or do if you were Alan's friend?

3. Why did Alan want to skip baseball practice right after the accident? Should he have told his mom the real reason?

4. Alan noticed a young boy watching him just after the accident. What do you think that boy was thinking about?

5. Alan's dad was driving when the accident happened. How do you think his dad felt about the accident? Would your answer change if you knew that his dad did or did not cause the accident?

6. Alan was hesitant to ride in a car after the accident. Why is it important to face your fears?

7. Alan's feelings about the accident seemed to change over time. Have you noticed that you can be very upset about something and then feel better about it later in time? What steps did Alan take to make that happen?

8. Why was Alan's sister, Maxine, so angry with Alan? Have you ever felt like Maxine felt? How should Alan's parents have helped Maxine in this situation?

9. Why was Alan uncertain about speaking with a psychologist? Have your parents ever asked you to talk to someone to help you with your feelings? If so, did you benefit from it in some way?

10. Alan noticed he was hurt, but not on the outside. What did he mean by that?

Other Chapter Books by Reflections Publishing:

The Real Beauty: Navigating Through Divorce and Moving
ISBN: 978-1-61660-000-6
Written by: Kathryn Mohr
Illustrated by: Kiana Aryan

Face 2 Face: Navigating Through Cyberbullying, Peer Abuse, & Bullying
ISBN: 978-1-61660-002-0
Written by: Caroline Ster
Illustrated by: Emily Jones

Scars: Navigating Through Peer Pressure & Consequences of Actions
ISBN: 978-1-61660-003-7
By Parent/Child Team: Dave, Julian, and Noelle Franco

Shining Through a Social Storm: Navigating Through Relational Aggression, Bullying, and Popularity
ISBN: 978-1-61660-004-4
Written by: Skylar Sorkin
Illustrated by: Sydney Green

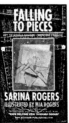

Falling to Pieces: Navigating the Transition to Middle School & Merging Friends
ISBN: 978-1-61660-007-5
Written by: Sarina Rogers
Illustrated by: Mia Rogers

Picture Books by Reflections Publishing:

Remind Me Again: Navigating Through the Loss of a Loved One
HC: ISBN: 978-1-61660-001-3
P: ISBN: 978-1-61660-010-5
Written by: The Ster Family
Illustrated by: Colleen C. Ster

A Mother's Love: Overcoming a Disability and Believing in Yourself
ISBN: 978-1-61660-008-2
Written by: Anthony Mazza
and Emmanuel Ofosu Yeboah

Remember Me When: Navigating Through Alzheimer's Disease
ISBN: 978-1-61660-009-9
Written by: Isabelle Ster
Illustrated by: Emily Morgan

Books Available through:
ReflectionsPublishing.com, amazon.com,
Follett Library Resources, Barnes and Noble,
Baker and Taylor, and Ingram.

CPSIA information can be obtained
at www.ICGtesting.com
Printed in the USA
FSOW02n1426290116
16313FS